Thomas R. (Thomas Robert) Way, H. B. Wheatley

Reliques of old London upon the Banks of the Thames & in the Suburbs south of the River

Thomas R. (Thomas Robert) Way, H. B. Wheatley

Reliques of old London upon the Banks of the Thames & in the Suburbs south of the River

ISBN/EAN: 9783337119522

Printed in Europe, USA, Canada, Australia, Japan

Cover: Foto ©ninafisch / pixelio.de

More available books at **www.hansebooks.com**

RELIQUES OF OLD LONDON UPON THE BANKS OF THE THAMES & IN THE SUBURBS SOUTH OF THE RIVER

DRAWN IN LITHOGRAPHY BY
T. R. WAY
WITH AN INTRODUCTION AND DESCRIPTIONS BY
H. B. WHEATLEY, F.S.A.

LONDON: GEORGE BELL AND SONS: MDCCCXCIX

PREFACE

THE present volume dealing with the old buildings along the River banks, and a few of the more remarkable houses of the past in the Surrey and Kentish suburbs, completes this series of volumes of Reliques of Old London. Yet the whole collection of ninety-six drawings forms but a small proportion of the subjects available for study by lovers of the past, for in the choice of subjects, I have been entirely guided by my own feelings as to the picturesqueness of the buildings and their surroundings, and have passed over many places which are of more importance from an historical point of view; so that this little gathering makes no claim to any sort of completeness as a record of the old buildings standing in London at this century's end. I have kept, as far as possible, to my original intention of only drawing private houses, which, as such, are liable to be pulled down at their owner's pleasure, and against whose destruction protest is useless; but in the present volume it will be noticed that amongst the river-side subjects are at least four which are public buildings, and so will probably be left undisturbed for all time. I felt, however, that these subjects, Greenwich Hospital, the Tower, Somerset House and Chelsea Hospital, were so intimately connected with the antiquities of the river front that I could not do otherwise than include them. And, indeed, so sweeping are the changes which are about to take place in the London of the past by the making of new roads, that no building seems safe. In 1896, when the drawing of Arch Row, Lincoln's Inn Fields, was made, few people dreamed that this delightful group of houses, almost entirely the work of Inigo Jones, would be handed over by Parliament to the tender mercies of the County Council; but the bill is passed, and unless something quite unforeseen happens, they will all disappear in a very few years. Let us hope that another architect will arise of an equal genius to Inigo Jones to replace them.

On a future occasion, I may perhaps publish another volume, uniform in size with the Reliques, dealing with the Royal palaces, and a few of the more important of the houses in central London, which I was unable to include in the first two volumes.

I wish to record my thanks to the many kind friends who have assisted me in various ways in collecting and producing these Reliques of our glorious old city, and especially to Mr. Wheatley for his invaluable collaboration.

T. R. WAY.

CONTENTS

	PLATE	PAGE
INTRODUCTION		1
Map of London, South of the Thames, 1815		14
THAMES-SIDE SUBJECTS:		
Greenwich Hospital	1	17
The Harbour Master, Limehouse	2	23
Cherry Garden	3	27
The Tower . . . . . (*Frontispiece*)	4	31
Somerset House	5	35
The Shot Towers	6	41
Lambeth Palace	7	45
Vauxhall Bridge	8	49
Chelsea Hospital	9	53
Old Battersea Bridge	10	57
Lindsay Row	11	61
Kew Bridge and Strand-on-the-Green . . .	12	65
SURREY SUBURBS:		
WIMBLEDON:		
Eagle House .	13	69
PUTNEY:		
No. 85, High Street .	14	73
WANDSWORTH:		
Albert House, South Street	15	77

	PLATE	PAGE
CLAPHAM:		
12 to 23, North Side, Clapham Common	16	81
TOOTING:		
Fairfield House	17	85
KENTISH SUBURBS:		
BROCKLEY:		
The Brockley Jack	18	89
LEWISHAM:		
Colfe's Almshouses	19	93
CHARLTON:		
Charlton House	20	97
BLACKHEATH:		
Morden College	21	101
GREENWICH:		
Ranger's Lodge	22	105
Croom's Hill and Stockwell Street	23	109
High Bridge	24	109

INTRODUCTION

FROM GREENWICH TO KEW BRIDGE

LONDON, from its position on the river Thames and its comparative nearness to the sea, has naturally become the great capital of the world.

The history of the river is full of interest, but this history cannot be disengaged from that of London itself. London grew up by the side of the river, and the northern bank has for many centuries been largely built upon, while those parts outside the City, on both banks, were dotted with villages both eastward and westward.

On the banks of the river within the City there were quays and busy landing places, with a few grim fortresses such as Barnard Castle and Coldharbour, inhabited by noblemen and royal personages.

To the east of London Bridge is the Tower, which guarded the City from that side; farther on were shipping villages as far as Greenwich and beyond; and here, as now, was a refuge for ships, which must always have been a busy and dirty neighbourhood.

On the other side of the bridge, from Blackfriars to Westminster, were a large number of waterside mansions with gardens which were beautiful to look upon. The river was the gayest and liveliest of thoroughfares, covered as it was with wherries and barges and all varieties of boats, a brilliant contrast to its dulness in the present day.

On the southern side there were not many buildings, and Southwark and Lambeth became the headquarters of pleasure seekers. Here were most of the theatres in Elizabethan and Jacobean times, and later on there were here many forms of public gardens. To all these places visitors were taken by the watermen who plied at all the stairs.

The monk Fitz Stephen, in his interesting description of the state of London in the twelfth century, gives an account of the water tournament and quintain, which must have occupied a good deal of room in the busy stream. He says, " In the Easter holidays they play at a game resembling a naval engagement. A target is firmly fastened to the trunk of a tree, which is fixed in the middle of the river, and in the prow of a boat driven along by oars and the current, stands a young man, who is to strike the target with his lance; if in hitting it he break his lance, and keep his position unmoved, he gains his point and attains his desire; but if his lance be not shivered by the blow, he is tumbled into the river, and his boat passes by, driven along by its own motion. Two boats, however, are placed there, one on each side of the target, and in them a number of young men to take up the striker, when he first emerges from the stream, or when

" A second time he rises from the wave."

On the bridge, and in balconies on the banks of the river, stand the spectators,

"... well disposed to laugh."

Those must have been gay times when kings and queens were to be seen among their subjects upon the water ; for the Thames was the royal road from Westminster and Whitehall to the Tower, and from thence to Greenwich.

The poet Gower probably lived at Southwark, and one day when he had taken boat he accidentally met the king (Richard II.) in his tapestried barge, who desired him to write a poem. This origin of the "Confessio Amantis" is thus explained in the original Prologue to the poem:

"As it befell upon a tide,
As thing, which shuldé tho betide,
Under the town of newé Troy,
Which toke of Brute his firsté joy,
In Themsé, whan it was flowend,
As I by boté came rowend
So as fortúne her timé sette,
My legé lord perchaunce I mette.
And so befell as I came nigh
Out of my bote, whan he me sigh,
He bad me come into his barge.
And whan I was with him at large,
Amongés other thingés said
He hath this charge upon me laid
And bad me do my businesse,
That to his highé worthynesse
Some newé thing I shuldé boke,
That he himself it mighté loke
After the forme of my writing
And thus upon his commaunding
Min herte is well the moré glad
To writé so as he me bad."

This was written in 1393, but when Richard's conduct had become past endurance Gower omitted these lines, and for

"In our Englishe I thenke make
A boké for King Richardes sake,"

he wrote

"A boké for Englondés sake."

3

Later on in the Prologue he expressed his allegiance to Henry of Lancaster.

Hall the chronicler tells the story of how the Archbishop of York led the widow of Edward IV. to the sanctuary of Westminster, and when he returned to York House at the dawning of day, he opened his windows and saw "the river full of boats of the Duke of Gloucester his servants watching that no person should go to Sanctuary nor none should pass unsearched."

When Henry VII.'s queen, Elizabeth of York, was to be crowned, she came from Greenwich, attended by "barges freshly furnished with banners and streamers of silk." In the next reign, when Henry VIII. avowed his marriage with Anne Boleyn, she was brought by all the crafts of London from Greenwich to the Tower," trumpets, shawms and other divers instruments, all the way playing and making great melody."

Queen Elizabeth was often on the river, and when she died at Richmond her body was brought with great pomp by water to Whitehall.

"The Queen was brought by water to Whitehall;
At every stroke, the oars did tears let fall."

On Charles I.'s creation as Prince of Wales in 1616, he came from Barn Elms to Whitehall in great aquatic state. In 1625, when Henrietta Maria arrived in London (June 16th), "the king and queen in the royal barge, with many other barges of honour and thousands of boats, passed through London Bridge to Whitehall; infinite numbers besides these, in wherries, standing in houses, ships, lighters, western barges, and on each side of the shore."[1]

Pepys was almost daily on the river, and tells in his Diary of many interesting occurrences, but one of the most striking of these is recorded on August 23rd, 1662, when the queen came from Hampton Court. There were so many people on the water that the Diarist could not get a boat, although he offered eight shillings for it. So he climbed to the top of the Banqueting House and had a fine view over the Thames. He writes, "All the show consisted chiefly in the number of boats and barges ; and two pageants, one of a king, and another of a queen with her maydes of honour sitting at her feet very prettily, and they tell me the queen is Sir Richard Ford's daughter. Anon come the King and Queen in a barge under a canopy, with 10,000 barges and boats, I think, *for we could see* no water for them, nor discern the King and Queen."

Strype, the historian and continuator of Stow's Survey, was told by a member of the Watermen's Company, that there were in his day 40,000 watermen on the rolls of the Company, and that upon occasion they could furnish 28,000 for the fleet, and that there were then 8,000 in service. These numbers may be exaggerated, but nevertheless the number of watermen needed to manage the boats mentioned by Pepys, must have been considerable.

[1] Ellis's *Letters*, First Series, vol. iii. p. 196.

All this is very charming, but there was another side to the picture. These watermen were very foul-mouthed, but it was much the fashion for the "gentry" to try to beat them with their own weapons. We know how Dr. Johnson once fought such a duel, and, in his heavy sledge-hammer style, he certainly scored a victory. Some called this "River Wit," but Addison in the "Spectator" more correctly styled it "Thames ribaldry." Pepys was never behindhand in the customs of his time, and he tells us how on May 14th, 1669, his wife, his brother and himself, went by water as high as Fulham, talking and singing, and playing the rogue with the western bargemen about the women of Woolwich, which mads them;" and on May 28th he was again making sport of the western bargees. Those comic but vulgar authors, Ned Ward and Tom Brown, paid particular attention to the watermen's dialect, and quoted their talk in its broadest form.

Mansions had their water-gates, and their owners had their own private barges, as had the citizens and the City Companies. The water-gate built for George Villiers, first Duke of Buckingham, as the entrance to his new palace, York House, is figured on the cover to this volume.[1]

Misson, in his interesting account of London, says of barges, "They give this name in England to a sort of

---

[1] There is a reference to this water-gate in the "Later Reliques of Old London," 1897. Plate XXI shows Buckingham Street with the gate at the bottom of the street.

pleasure boat, at one end of which is a little room handsomely painted and cover'd, with a table in the middle and benches round it; and at the other end seats for 8, 10, 12, 30 or 40 rowers. There are very few persons of great quality but what have their barges, tho' they do not frequently make use of them. Their watermen wear a jacket of the same colour they give for their livery, with a pretty large silver badge upon their arm, with the nobleman's coat of arms emboss'd in it. These watermen have some privileges as belonging to peers; but they have no wages, are not domestick servants. They live in their own houses with their families and earn their livelihood as they can. The Lord Mayor of London, and the several Companies have also their barges, and are carry'd in them upon certain solemn occasions."

It is said that the last Primate who kept his state barge at Lambeth Palace was Archbishop Wake, who died in 1737.

The first Lord Mayor's water pageant was due to John Norman, Mayor in 1454, who is described by Fabyan as "the first of all the mayors who brake that ancient and old continued custom of *riding* to Westminster upon the morrow of Simon and Jude's day." For this the watermen held him in high honour, and sang a roundel beginning:

"Row the boat, Norman, row to thy leman."

The Companies, however, had their barges for water processions half a century before this, and the Grocers' accounts, temp. Henry VI., mention the hiring of barges to attend the Sheriffs' show by water. When the Thames resembled the Grand Canal at Venice in life and beauty the water was pure; the river was full of fish and salmon was plentiful. Swans were seen in large quantities, and Paulus Jovius (died 1552) wrote, "This river abounds in swans swimming in flocks; the sight of whom and their noise is agreeable to the fleets that meet them in their course."

When boats were to be had at all the stairs, men and women felt little need of bridges for crossing the river, and London Bridge for many years was found sufficient for the carts and other conveyances that went from the City to Southwark; but in the seventeenth century there was a strong feeling in the West End that the time had come for the building of some other bridges. The City, however, successfully prevented the carrying out of any such wishes. On April 4th, 1671, a bill was brought into the House of Commons for building a bridge over the river Thames from Putney. Mr. Jones (M.P. for London) said the building of another bridge would ruin London. Sir William Thompson catalogued the evils that the proposed bridge would bring about, and Mr. Love said if carts went over it the City must be destroyed by it. Of those in favour of the scheme Waller, the poet, said, "We are still obstructing things," and Colonel Stroude said, "In no city where bridges are were they all built at a time. No city in the world is so long as ours, and here is but one passage for five miles." The bill was rejected by 67 to 54.[1]

The first bridge to be built, and thus destroy the uniqueness of London Bridge, was Putney Bridge in 1729; Westminster Bridge followed in 1739-50, Blackfriars in 1760-69 and Battersea Bridge in 1772. No more bridges were built in the eighteenth century. Vauxhall Bridge was built in 1811-16, Waterloo Bridge in 1811-17, Southwark Bridge in 1815-19, Hungerford Suspension Bridge in 1846 (superseded by Charing Cross Bridge in 1863), Chelsea Suspension Bridge in 1856-58, Lambeth Bridge in 1862-63, Albert Bridge, Chelsea, in 1873 and the Tower Bridge in 1886-94.

In the present century the special interest of the river above London Bridge gradually died out, the number of boats became less and less, the gardens, except in a few cases, were built over or passed out of cultivation, the condition of the river at low water became worse and worse, until in the second half of the century the Embankment of the river was undertaken, and the Thames again became the chief ornament of London.

[1] Grey's "Debates of the House of Commons."

THE SUBURBS SOUTH OF THE RIVER.

THE southern suburbs are of very great interest, but they can scarcely be considered so full of literary and historical associations as those on the north side of the river, in spite of the many royal residences which once existed in South London.

Up to the middle of the present century the south was more rural than the north, but in the latter half of the century the former has increased in number of inhabitants at a much greater rate than the latter, and in South London there is perhaps more sordid poverty and a thicker population than in almost any part on the north of the Thames.

The southern suburbs are fortunate in the possession of a matchless series of open spaces. Few, if any towns can boast of such a stretch of charming country as that which includes Wimbledon, Barnes, Wandsworth and Clapham Commons and Putney Heath. Here the beauties of the lovely county of Surrey are brought to the very doors of the town. In Kent we have Greenwich Park and Blackheath, and many important relics of the past.

Many of the interesting old buildings of southern London have disappeared of late, but every Londoner must be proud that so fine a mansion as Charlton House, which reminds us of the grandest period of Domestic Architecture, still remains.

The Common land and open country, which is so

delightful to us in the nineteenth century, had its disadvantages in the eighteenth and earlier centuries as the happy hunting grounds of highwaymen or gentlemen of the road.

A wonderful amount of romantic nonsense has grown up around the history of highwaymen. These men received an immense amount of sympathy in circles far beyond the range of their own acquaintances, but an inquiry into the facts of the lives of such men as Claude Duval and Dick Turpin leaves little to make us understand the admiration felt by women for these heroes.

The origin of the feeling of admiration is doubtless to be found in the fact that highwaymen stand apart from ordinary thieves in being the lineal descendants of the outlaw knights and the brigands of earlier centuries. There was a certain amount of wrongly directed bravery required in their pursuits, and this is always admired in an unsettled state of society.

Highway robbery was in a flourishing condition during the latter part of the eighteenth century, but highwaymen themselves fell lower and lower in social position. Mails were robbed and coaches were stopped, but as trade increased and a better system of police was established the occupation became unprofitable and died out. Not only were the means of prevention improved, but the facilities for robbery were less. With the increase of banking, and the improved methods of trading, coin and other valuables were not carried about the person by travellers.

Most of the stories of the courtesy of highwaymen are lies, but there are a few instances of gentlemen who, having run through their property, took to the road. Parsons, the son of a baronet, was educated at Eton, and for a short time was in the navy. He ran through his money, and being desperate, owing to his debts, became a highwayman. After many adventures he was captured, tried and hanged in 1750.

The thought of the inevitable end of the highwayman, must have forced itself upon his mind, for while other criminals escaped, he always came to the gallows at last. We read a good deal about honour among thieves, but little of this appears in real life. Ned Ward, who drew a vivid picture of the typical highwayman, gives no hint of its existence. He writes, "He's as generous as a prince, treats anybody that will keep him company; loves his friends as dearly as the ivy does the oak, will never leave him till he has hug'd him to his ruin. He has drawn in twenty of his associates to be hang'd, but had always wit and money enough to save his own neck from the halter."

The thief-takers let him pass, and the ostlers helped with business, until he was down on his luck, when he was given over to justice. Highwaymen were to be found in all parts of the southern suburbs, but their chief resort for several centuries was Shooter's Hill. The road there was steep and narrow, and was closed in by thick woods, which formed a shelter for robbers. As early as the reign of Richard II. the need of improvement was acknowledged;

Henry IV. "granted leave to Thomas Chapman to cut down, burn and sell all the woods and underwoods growing and confining to Shooter's Hill, on the south side, and to bestow the money raised thereby upon mending the highway." The road, however, was not improved.

Oldham wrote in 1682.

> "Hither in flocks from Shooter's Hill they come,
> To seek their prize and booty nearer home:
> 'Your purse!' they cry; 'tis madness to resist
> Or strive, with cock'd pistol at your breast."

When the highwaymen were caught they were hanged on the gibbet, and travellers usually found one at least hanging there. Pepys and Mrs. Anne rode under the gibbet with its ghastly prey on April 11th, 1661.

An improved road was made about 1733, but the highwayman still made Shooter's Hill his headquarters.

Byron made Don Juan shoot a highwayman who assaulted him here with the cry, "Your money or your life!"

> "Don Juan had got out on Shooter's Hill,
> Sunset the time, the place the same declivity
> Which looks along that vale of good and ill
> Where London's streets ferment in full activity."

How changed is now the scene. There is nothing to tell the inhabitants of the modern villas that they live where once these deeds of blood were enacted.

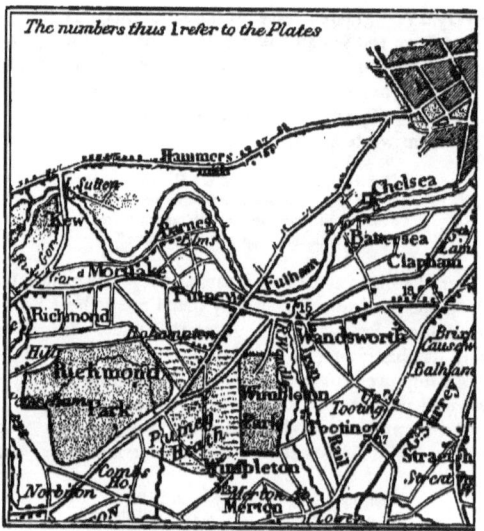

MAP OF THE ENVIRONS OF LONDON.

The above map is the lower half of that used in the Volume of "Suburban Reliques of Old London, North of the Thames." It has been enlarged from a map in an old guide book of the early part of the century. It shows a

(Taken from "The Original Picture of London," and dated 1815.)

curious incompleteness in the number of bridges drawn. Even old Battersea Bridge, which was built in 1772, is not marked.

Plate 1

PLATE I

GREENWICH HOSPITAL

GREENWICH was for several centuries intimately associated with our kings and queens, and there is a reference to a royal residence here as early as the reign of Edward I., but little is recorded of the place before the time of Henry IV. The latter king made it his favourite residence, and dated his will from his manor of Greenwich.

Henry V. granted the manor for life to his uncle, Thomas Beaufort, Duke of Exeter, and on the death of the latter in 1427 it was granted to Henry V.'s brother, Humphrey, Duke of Gloucester, who formed Greenwich Park, and built a tower known as Greenwich Castle, which stood on the site of the Royal Observatory. He also commenced to build the palace of Placentia.

On the duke's death the manor reverted to the crown and Edward IV. made a considerable enlargement of the palace. In 1465 he settled the manor and town of Greenwich and the park on his queen, Elizabeth Woodville. This unfortunate woman was confined in the Bermondsey Abbey by Henry VII., and died there in poverty. Henry VII. made many additions to the palace, and finished the tower in the park begun by Duke Humphrey. Henry VIII. was born at Greenwich and baptized in the parish church. This king was attracted to the place by his love of ships, and the great fame of Greenwich dates from his time. Many of the most important incidents of his reign occurred here, and here his great successor, Elizabeth, was born.

Edward VI. kept his Christmas at Greenwich in 1552, and died here on July 2nd, 1553. Elizabeth kept her court here and made several additions to the palace. In the Sutherland Collection at the Bodleian Library there is a drawing of the palace of Placentia by Van der Wyngaerde showing a long stretch of low buildings close by the river bank, as it appeared in the reigns of Henry VIII. and Elizabeth. James I. and Charles I. both held their courts at Greenwich, but after the Restoration Charles II. found the palace so much out of repair owing to neglect during the Commonwealth period, that he ordered it to be taken down. The king then commenced the erection of a new palace of freestone. Sir John Denham was the surveyor-general, but the architect employed was Webb, the son-in-law of Inigo Jones, from whose papers the designs were made. One wing was completed at a cost of £36,000, which afterwards formed the west wing of the Royal Hospital; little, however, remains, as most of it was burnt and then rebuilt. Charles occasionally resided here, but the building was chiefly used for the Navy Office, and for the sick and wounded in the Dutch wars, who were under the care of John Evelyn.

To the charitable instincts of Queen Mary we owe the formation of Greenwich Hospital. The letters patent granting to commissioners certain lands and " all that capital messauge lately built or in building by our royall uncle King Charles II., and still remaining unfinished, commonly called by the name of our Palace of Greenwich," to erect and found a hospital " for the reliefe and support of Seamen serving on board the shipps or vessells belonging to the Navy Royall," are dated October 25th, 1694, and the Queen died on December 28th of the same year. Sir Christopher Wren undertook the office of architect without pay, and he built himself a house on the east side of Greenwich Park to be his residence during the progress of the building. Sir John Vanbrugh was his surveyor, and he has left his name in Vanbrugh Castle and Vanbrugh Park.

The hospital is original in design and equally effective in appearance. It consists of four distinct blocks; on either side of the great square facing the river are two blocks, King Charles's

Plate 2

PLATE II

THE HARBOUR MASTER, LIMEHOUSE

THE banks of the Thames have been greatly altered of late years, but, in spite of these changes, some old spots still remain to show us what the waterside was like of old. There is a specially quaint appearance about the house of the Harbour Master of the Port of London shown in this picture, and the title itself has a distinctly old-world flavour. Limehouse is a genuine relic of an old boating centre, and its name tells of the time when the lime-kilns or lime-hostes were the chief features of the place. Part of the main riverside road was long known as Lime-kiln Hill.

Samuel Pepys was a frequent visitor to Limehouse, and on October 19th, 1661, he went to Captain Marsh's, at a house which had been in his family for two hundred and fifty years, "close by the limehouse which gives the name to the place." He adds in his Diary that there was a design to get the king to hire a dock for the herring busses. On December 3rd, 1662, he again visited Limehouse to see the herring boats then being built, "that being a thing we are now very hot upon." On September 7th, 1664, he went to Mr. Margetts, the rope merchant, to see his ropeyard there, with the intention of employing him for the government. Earlier than these references is one on March 23rd, 1659-60, when Pepys went with his patron, Sir Edward Montagu, in a barge to Long Reach, where the "Swiftsure" was at anchor, and we are told how in his way he saw the great breach which high water had made, to the loss of many thousands of pounds to the people of Limehouse.

Shakespeare refers to the chapel audiences of "Tribulation of

Tower Hill," and of "the Limb of Limehouse" in "King Henry VIII.," act v., scene 3.

Limehouse is on the Middlesex bank of the Thames, between Wapping and Poplar. It was originally a hamlet of Stepney, and was first made a distinct parish in 1730.

Dickens refers to Limehouse Hole (at the far end of Limehouse) as the dwelling-place of Rogue Riderhood and his daughter Pleasant in "Our Mutual Friend."

Dick Shore, now Duck Shore, Limehouse, is a landing-place or stairs, at the Narrow Street end of Fore Street, not far from the great turn of the river southward, opposite to the Isle of Dogs.

Limehouse Church is one of the finest churches in the East-end, and is seen to advantage from many parts round about. It is one of fifty churches erected in the reign of Queen Anne, and was designed by Nicholas Hawksmoor, a pupil of Wren.

Plate 3

PLATE III

CHERRY GARDEN

THERE is something incongruous to our present ideas in the fact that cherry trees grew by the banks of the Thames in the parish of Rotherhithe, two centuries ago.

The "Cherry Garden" was a favourite place of public entertainment in the reign of Charles II., and we know that that rural name was not mis-applied as we have the authority of Pepys for saying that cherries grew in the gardens, and that on June 13th, 1664, the Diarist picked some and carried them home.

The site of the gardens is marked by Cherry Garden stairs, a landing pier for Thames steamers and small boats. Rotherhithe is a manor and parish on the Surrey side of the Thames between Bermondsey and Deptford. It is not mentioned in Domesday Book, as it was then a hamlet in the royal manor of Bermondsey.

It has been stated that the famous Admiral Benbow was born in Rotherhithe, but this is a mistake, as he was born at Coton Hill, Shrewsbury. We learn, however, from Dean Swift that Lemuel Gulliver was long an inhabitant of the place, and that it was a sort of proverb among his neighbours at Redriff, that "it was as true as if Mr. Gulliver had spoken it." Rotherhithe is closely associated with Turner's grand picture, "The Fighting Téméraire tugged to her last berth to be broken up, 1838," for there, at the shipbreaking yard then in the occupation of Mr. John Beatson, was the last berth of the old ship.

The figure-heads of various old ships of the Fleet adorned the entrance gates of the yard in Rotherhithe Street, and were the subject of the famous picture entitled "Old Friends," by the late H. S. Marks, R.A., which was shown in the Royal Academy Exhibition of 1879.

PLATE IV

THE TOWER

THERE is no other building on the banks of the Thames of such transcendent interest as the Tower of London, which may be considered as the very embodiment of English history for several centuries.

The White Tower, with its four corner turrets, is one of the most familiar objects to those who journey along the Thames, but although it contains the oldest portions of the old fortress, the exterior was so modernized by Sir Christopher Wren that a single window, through which Bishop Flambard is said to have escaped from imprisonment in the reign of Henry I., alone remains to tell of the Norman origin of the Tower. Within, however, is preserved in St. John's Chapel one of the finest examples of Norman ecclesiastical building in the country.

The points of interest connected with the Tower are very many, but the chief features of its history are included in the records of its use as a fortress, a palace, and a prison.

Although in the present condition of warfare the Tower could not stand a siege, it is practically a fortress still, as it has been for nine centuries. The Tower was used as a palace until after the Restoration. The early kings used it constantly, and it was naturally considered as their strongest fortress, but in later and more settled times its gloominess became distasteful, and it was only occupied by the sovereign just before his coronation. Charles II. was the last king to use it in this manner.

Many of the most interesting incidents in the history of England took place in the Tower. Soon after the accession of Richard II. some of the most fearful scenes during the Peasants'

Revolt were acted here, and here the unhappy king delivered up his crown to Henry IV. The mediæval notions of a palace and a prison were intimately associated, and therefore there is nothing incongruous in thinking of the Tower as a prison just after considering it as a palace. One of the early prisoners was Charles, Duke of Orleans, father of Louis XII., who has left a record of his imprisonment in the earliest view of the Tower preserved in the library of the British Museum. Everyone looks with interest on the Tower as the prison-house of some of the noblest and greatest of our land, but it is impossible here even to find room for a bare list of these noble men and women.

There were two places of execution for the prisoners: one on Tower Hill, under the jurisdiction of the Lord Mayor and citizens, and the other on Tower Green, within the walls, in front of the Chapel of St. Peter ad Vincula.

The Traitors' Gate was one of the entrances to the Tower, but it was only used for the reception of prisoners of rank. It still remains, but the embankment in front of it has destroyed its character as a water-gate. The poet Rogers refers to it in his "Human Life":

> "On through that gate mis-named, through which before
> Went Sidney, Russell, Raleigh, Cranmer, More."

That portion of the Tower which chiefly interested our forefathers was the menagery. The Lion Tower stood on the site of the present entrance, just without the Middle Tower. Henry I. kept lions and leopards, and Henry III. added to the collection. The Tower menagery was one of the sights of London up to the reign of William IV., from which the expression "seeing the lions" originated.

Plate 5

PLATE V

SOMERSET HOUSE

SOMERSET House, with the Embankment gardens fronting the Adelphi, and Waterloo Bridge in the foreground, forms the most picturesque point on the riverside of London. It is seen at its best from Charing Cross Bridge, partly because on this bridge we only notice the beauty of the view and are not disturbed by the obtrusive ugliness of the railway bridge.

There has been a Somerset House here since the reign of Edward VI., when the king's uncle, the Protector Somerset, built the first house and made many enemies for himself by his undertaking. His palace, which was afterwards appropriated to queens consort, was pulled down in 1775, and the present building was erected between 1776 and 1786, after the designs of Sir William Chambers. Fortunately Chambers foresaw the eventual embanking of the Thames, and he built it in accordance with this belief, so that it fits in with the present scheme. The building is in the form of a quadrangle with wings. The Strand front is 155 feet long, and the river front 600 feet. The inner quadrangle is 319 by 224 feet. Wings have been added to Chambers's building; the east wing, which contains King's College, by Sir R. Smirke in 1828-31; the west wing, devoted to the Inland Revenue Department, by Sir James Pennethorne in 1853.

Somerset House has been intimately associated with the Science, the Art and the Government of the country. Some of the greatest scientific men of the last and present centuries—the Herschels and Watt, Davy and Wollaston, visited the rooms of the Royal Society, and at the Royal Academy, within the period it was located there (1780 and 1838), Reynolds discoursed, and with

Wilkie, Flaxman, Chantrey and many other artists exhibited. An old clerk at the Audit Office told the late Peter Cunningham the following interesting incident of the courtyard. "When I first came to this building," he said, "I was in the habit of seeing for many mornings a thin, spare, naval officer, with only one arm, enter the vestibule at a smart step, and make direct for the Admiralty, over the rough round stones of the quadrangle instead of taking what others generally took, and continue to take, the smooth pavement at the sides. His thin, frail figure shook at every step, and I often wondered why he chose so rough a footway; but I ceased to wonder when I heard that the thin, frail officer was no other than Lord Nelson—who always took the nearest way to the place he wanted to go to."

The Victoria Embankment was commenced in 1862 and opened by the Prince of Wales in 1870. One of the arches of Waterloo Bridge now spans the embankment instead of the slime of the river.

Waterloo Bridge, which has been greatly admired, and described as "the finest bridge in Europe," is beautiful from the charm of its proportions. Dupin, the great French engineer, called it "a colossal monument worthy of Sesostris and the Cæsars," and Canova said that it alone was worth coming from Rome to London to see. The first intention of the projector was to erect a wooden bridge, and when enough money was obtained by tolls to build a stone one. The proposal was successfully opposed in three successive sessions of Parliament, but an act for a stone bridge was obtained in 1809. The proprietors were incorporated under the title of the Strand Bridge Company, with power to raise £500,000, subsequently increased from time to time, and ultimately above one million sterling was expended upon the work.

John Rennie was the architect, and two designs were furnished for the proposed bridge, the one with seven and the other with nine arches, and the latter was adopted.

The first stone was laid on October 11th, 1811, when a block of Cornish granite was lowered over an excavation containing gold and silver coins of the realm, with a suitable inscription.

The foundations were laid in cofferdams, and blocks of Craigleith and Derbyshire granite were used for the piers, abutment and entire superstructure. There are a series of arches on each side which raise the road to the level of the bridge. Thirty-nine are on the Surrey side, each of sixteen feet span in addition to one of larger dimensions crossing the road below. There are sixteen arches on the Strand side. The total length of the bridge, including the brick arches, is 2,456 feet.

The reasons for the change of name of the bridge are thus given in the Act of Parliament of 1816: "Whereas the said bridge, when completed, will be a work of great stability and magnificence, and such works are adapted to transmit to posterity the remembrance of great and glorious achievements, and whereas the Company of proprietors are desirous that a designation shall be given to the said bridge which shall be a lasting record of the brilliant and decisive victory achieved by his Majesty's forces, in conjunction with those of his allies, on the 18th day of June, 1815."

Plate 6

PLATE VI

THE SHOT TOWERS

THE two Shot Towers shown in this drawing are very striking objects on the south side of the river, but they have not received, in the ordinary books about London, the attention they deserve. Both existed before Waterloo Bridge was built, and they mark the confines of the notorious Cuper's Gardens, through which the Waterloo Road was cut.

The square tower to the east was built soon after 1782, when a workman named Watts, residing at Bristol, discovered a new process of shot manufacture. In the old method the lead was dropped so short a distance before touching the water, that the shot was seldom of a satisfactorily spherical shape.

Watts conceived the notion of letting the lead fall from a great height into the water, so that it might cool and harden in a spherical form during its passage through the air, and not receive any change of shape on its sudden contact with the water. The story is told that the idea came to him in a dream, and that he tried the feasibility of his idea by pouring some melted lead from the tower of the church of St. Mary, Redcliffe. Watts patented his process, and sold the right to work his patent to some persons who had money, which he had not. The eastern of the two towers was built, and the shot-making firm traded under the name of Messrs. Watts.

Messrs. Watts were succeeded by Messrs. Walker. The height of the tower from the ground to the top of the turret is about 140 feet, and the shot fell 123 feet 6 inches. Early in the present century the western Shot Tower, which was of considerably greater height, was built by one Maltby. Some time after this the Walkers joined Maltby in the new manufactory, and the old tower was continued in work by Burns of Shrewsbury, and afterwards by Lane and Nesham.

The new tower was used by Messrs. Walker and Parker, and when this firm became a limited company they bought the old tower and carried on business at both. A few years ago, however, it was found that there was no need for two towers, and the square tower was let to Messrs. Dewar, for the storage of their whiskeys. This is situated in the Commercial Road, and the wharf where it stands is named the Old Shot Tower Wharf.

The Shot Tower in the foreground is situated in the Belvedere Road, which was formerly known as Narrow Walk, but re-named after the Belvedere House and Gardens, Lambeth. The amount of work done in this tower may be guessed by the knowledge of the fact that about 300,000 shot are made per minute. This is not the place to give an account of shot manufacture, but it may be said that there is a furnace at the top of the tower, and the melted lead is poured through a sort of sieve, and the shot falls through the centre of the tower to the bottom.[1]

[1] An article in the "Strand Magazine," vol. ii. (1891) pp. 205-209, entitled "Up a Shot Tower," contains an account of the manufacture at the tower in Belvedere Road, but no history of the towers is there given.

Plate 7

PLATE VII

LAMBETH PALACE

LAMBETH is a place of some antiquity and the Manor House, or Lambeth Palace, has been the residence of the Archbishops of Canterbury from the end of the twelfth century, when Archbishop Hubert Fitzwalter, in 1197, exchanged the Manor of Dartford, Kent, with Gilbert de Glanvill, Bishop of Rochester, for the manor and advowson of Lambeth.

Lambeth house was put up for sale in 1648, and purchased with the manor for £7,073 0s. 8d. by Thomas Scot and Matthew Hardy. The former was Secretary of State to the Protector, and one of the persons who sat on the trial of Charles I., for which he was executed at Charing Cross in 1660. Scot removed the tomb of Archbishop Parker, the leaden coffin was sold to a plumber, and the Archbishop's body was thrown into a hole in one of the outhouses. After the Restoration the body was discovered and re-interred in the chapel. Scot also turned the chapel into a dancing room.

Lambeth Palace is one of the most important old houses in London, but the various buildings are of very unequal interest. The oldest part is the chapel which was built by Boniface, Archbishop of Canterbury (1244-1270). The Hall was built on the site and of the proportions of the older hall by Archbishop Juxon, and has over the door his arms and the date 1663. This Hall was altered for the accommodation of the Library by Archbishop Howley. The whole of that part of the palace which forms the residence of the Archbishop was erected (1829-1834) by Archbishop Howley.

The church of St. Mary, Lambeth, whose tower is shown in

this picture is of no particular interest, as it was rebuilt by Hardwick. The Perpendicular tower was built soon after 1377. It has been restored, and remains as a relic of the old church. Those early naturalists and antiquaries, the Tradescant family, lived in South Lambeth, and there is a tomb in the churchyard, erected in 1662 and repaired in 1773, with an inscription commencing,

"Know stranger, ere thou pass beneath this stone
Lye John Tradescant, grandsire, father, son."

The museum of the Tradescants (usually called Tradeskin by their contemporaries) was very famous in its time, and Flatman, in one of his poems, thus mentions the Tradescant collection:

"Thus John Tradeskin starves our wondering eyes
By boxing up his new-born rarities."

The old Lambeth Bridge was only a landing-place for passengers and goods, and when the sovereign passed by in his barge it was the custom for the archbishop to resort to the bridge to pay his respects. On this bridge on the night of Sunday, December 9th, 1688, the Queen of James II., crossing by the ferry in her flight from Whitehall, landed with the infant prince, and had to shelter for a time under the shadow of Lambeth Church from the storm which raged.

A very ugly suspension bridge, leading from Church Street, Lambeth, to Horseferry Road, exactly on the line of the old Horse-ferry or Lambeth ferry, was erected in 1862 from the designs of Mr. P. W. Barlow, and opened in November, 1863. This bridge is condemned, and we may hope that it will be replaced by something more in harmony with the old buildings at Lambeth and the new Palace at Westminster.

Plate 8

PLATE VIII

VAUXHALL BRIDGE

AS the streets of London progressed towards the west on both sides of the river, the want of more bridge accommodation became evident, and at the beginning of the present century a new iron bridge was constructed, in spite of the opposition of the City. The original proposer was Ralph Dodd, the projector of tunnels. The work of construction was carried out by a body of shareholders, who employed Sir Samuel Bentham and John Rennie besides Dodd, but in spite of the employment of these distinguished men, the design of the bridge really belongs to James Walker.

The work was commenced on May 9th, 1811, the first stone being laid by Lord Dundas, acting as proxy for the Prince Regent. There seems to have been some delay in the proceedings, for more than two years elapsed (September, 1813) before the first stone of the abutments on the Surrey side was laid by Prince Charles, eldest son of the Duke of Brunswick, who was killed at the battle of Waterloo. The entire work was finished in 1816, at an expense of about £300,000, and was opened on June 4th.

The cast-iron superstructure with its nine arches was supported on rusticated stone piers. The arches were each 78 feet in span. The roadway measured 36 feet across, and the entire length of the bridge was 809 feet. When the bridge was finished, it was said to be the lightest structure of the kind in Europe.

It was first called Regent's Bridge, but the name was afterwards changed to Vauxhall Bridge on account of its nearness to Vauxhall Gardens. The bridge had been in an unsatisfactory condition for some time, and it was cleared away in 1899 and the new bridge commenced.

The designer of the new bridge is Sir A. Binnie, engineer to the London County Council, and its cost is estimated at £390,000. Now that Millbank has been rebuilt and a branch of the National Gallery has been opened there (the Tate Gallery), the want of a good bridge at this point is evident to all.

Plate 9

PLATE IX

CHELSEA HOSPITAL

THE two great institutions—for the support of old and disabled soldiers and sailors—are both ornaments to the riverside, and both had Wren for their architect; but it would be difficult to find two buildings more unlike. Chelsea Hospital is a charming old-fashioned mansion of red brick with stone dressings, having a centre and two wings. It has been said that this building shows more effect with less means than any other of Wren's secular buildings, but there are little or no marks of originality about it. On the other hand Greenwich Hospital is singularly original in conception, and we may therefore guess that Vanbrugh, who was an original genius, had a considerable hand in the plan of Greenwich.

The first building on the site was "King James's College," at Chelsea, founded in 1610 by Dr. Matthew Sutcliffe, Dean of Exeter, "to the intent that learned men might there have maintenance to aunswere all the adversaries of religion." This attempt to form a sort of headquarters of religious controversies was not very successful, and after Sutcliffe's death the place gradually decayed. Archbishop Laud called it "Controversy College."

After the Restoration the College was given to the Royal Society by the king, but it was not made use of, and in 1682 the king bought it back for £1,300, and the building of the hospital was proceeded with. Charles II. was the founder, but to Sir Stephen Fox and John Evelyn the idea of the foundation was largely due. Fox strongly urged the need of such an institution on the king.

There is a tradition that Nell Gwyn suggested the foundation of the hospital, but neither contemporary evidence, nor official records give any corroboration to this tradition, although there is still a long-established public-house with the sign of "Nell Gwynne," in the Pimlico Road.

The Royal Hospital accommodates 540 in-pensioners, and the out-pensioners are said to number nearly 70,000. Parliament makes an annual grant of about £24,000 for the support of the hospital. The buildings contain much of interest, and are intimately associated with many distinguished men. The body of the great Duke of Wellington lay in state in the Chapel previous to its interment in St. Paul's.

The grounds leading down to the river are well kept and pleasant to look upon. They were the scene of two of the most interesting exhibitions ever arranged in London, viz., the Military Exhibition in 1890, and the Naval Exhibition in 1891.

The hospital is still known in the neighbourhood as "The College."

Plate 10

PLATE X

OLD BATTERSEA BRIDGE

OLD Battersea Bridge (leading from Chelsea to Battersea), a rude timber structure of nineteen spans which took the place of a ferry, was for more than a century a great obstruction to the navigation of the river, and with old Putney Bridge, which was equally inconvenient and nearly half a century older, was long the terror of boating men.

The bridge was built in 1771-72, under an Act of Parliament obtained in 1766, at the expense of fifteen proprietors who subscribed £1,500 apiece, Mr. Holland being the designer.

The spans varied in width from 15 feet 6 inches to 32 feet, and when the bridge was acquired by the company which erected the Albert Bridge in 1873, four of the original spans were thrown into two; one of the enlarged spans measured 75 feet 3 inches, and the other 70 feet. These openings will be noticed in the drawing.

The greatest width of road was 23 feet 9 inches, but in parts the carriage way was only about 16 feet. The footpath on the up river side was in places only 2 feet wide, and on the down river side from 4 feet to 5 feet wide.

The bridge was purchased by the Metropolitan Board of Works in 1878 and condemned as unsafe in 1881. Under the sanction of an Act of Parliament (1881) a temporary footbridge was erected. The contract for this, and for the pulling down of the old bridge, was let to Messrs. Mowlem in 1885 for £7,153.

The present bridge was erected to the east of the old bridge. It is a cast-iron structure upon stone pillars, of five spans, the centre being 173 feet wide, and the width of the roadway is 40 feet. The cost of the bridge was £143,000.

The Metropolitan Board of Works having been superseded by the London County Council, the bridge was opened in July, 1890, by the Earl of Rosebery.

The Manor of Battersea, which before the Conquest belonged to Earl Harold, was given by the Conqueror to Westminster Abbey, in exchange for Windsor. After the dissolution of the monasteries, it was reserved for the Crown. In 1627 it was granted in reversion to Sir Oliver St. John, Viscount Grandison, and the manor remained in the St. John family until 1763, when it was sold to Earl Spencer. The residence of the great Lord Bolingbroke gave a distinction to the place.

Bolingbroke House was to the east of the church, and one of the interesting circumstances connected with it was the burning on the lawn of the 500 copies of the " Patriot King," about the printing of which so much mystery was made by Bolingbroke and Pope. The greater part of Bolingbroke House was demolished in 1778, only the wing being left which contained the circular room, wainscoted with cedar, popularly known as Pope's study. The memory of the house which has entirely disappeared, is preserved in Bolingbroke Road and Bolingbroke Terrace. Battersea Church, an ugly building which replaced in 1776-77 an older church, contains a monument with medallions by Roubiliac to Henry St. John Viscount Bolingbroke and his second wife Marie Clara des Champs de Maurily, niece of Madame de Maintenon. The other great house at Battersea was York House, whose memory is preserved in the names of York Terrace and York Road.

Lawrence Booth, Bishop of Durham in 1460, purchased an estate at Battersea, which, on his elevation to the Archbishopric of York, he presented to that see, and built on it a mansion as an occasional residence for himself and his successors when called to visit London. The last Archbishop who occupied York House was Archbishop Holgate who was deprived and imprisoned by Queen Mary for being a married man.

PLATE XI

LINDSAY ROW

THIS handsome block of fine red-brick houses stands close to the Chelsea end of Battersea Bridge, and is now included in Cheyne Walk. It was originally built as one house by Robert Bertie, third Earl of Lindsay, Lord Great Chamberlain about 1668, and the two end houses, forming wings to the entire block, project slightly and are ornamented with stone dressings.

The site was originally occupied by a house built by the celebrated Sir Theodore Mayerne, physician to James I. and Charles I., who also lived in St. Martin's Lane. He died at Chelsea, March 22nd, 1654-55, and was buried in St. Martin's churchyard. There is a fine portrait of Mayerne at the Royal College of Physicians.

Lord Lindsay bought the old house and rebuilt it. During his lifetime it was occupied by the notorious Duchess of Mazarin, niece of the Cardinal (1694-99), one of the most prominent beauties of Charles II.'s court, and here the popular litterateur, St. Evremond, was domiciled in her house.

Subsequently Lindsay House was occupied by Francis Lord Conway, and his son Francis Seymour Conway, Marquis of Hertford (cousin of Horace Walpole), was born here in 1719.

Count Zinzendorf determined in 1750 to form a Moravian centre in England, and in 1751 he purchased Lindsay House, and obtained from Sir Hans Sloane the gardens of Beaufort House for a graveyard. The stables of the same house he turned into a chapel. The brethren who inhabited Lindsay House were mostly missionaries, for whom it was intended that this should be a kind of "pilgrim house" and temporary home. Count Zinzendorf resided here as long as he remained in England. When subsequently the mansion was divided into five houses, the large house in the centre was named Lindsay House, and became the residence of Henry Constantine Jennings, generally known as "Dog Jennings," the celebrated connoisseur, who here preserved his magnificent collections which he ruined himself by collecting.

The house was afterwards occupied by the eminent engineers Brunel, father and son, and subsequently by Bramah, the inventor of the hydraulic press, and by John Martin, the painter.

In later days Mr. Whistler lived at No. 96, the easternmost house.

Plate 12

PLATE XII

KEW BRIDGE

THE original Kew Bridge, designed by John Barnard, was built about the year 1757, in pursuance of an Act of Parliament 30 Geo. II., by Robert Tunstall, the owner of the ferry between Brentford and Kew. It was a wooden bridge, and was finished in 1759, but it does not appear to have been very satisfactorily built, for it was soon found to require extensive repairs. Robert Tunstall, son of the former owner, therefore applied to Parliament for authority to build a new bridge in place of the old one. An Act of Parliament was passed and the first stone was laid June 4th, 1783. Kew Bridge is a stone structure of seven arches, and several smaller brick arches on the lower Surrey shore. The length is 400 feet exclusive of the abutments. The bridge was designed by James Paine, and built at the cost of Robert Tunstall. It was opened for public use on September 22nd, 1789, and was subsequently bought for £22,000 by G. Robinson. It continued private property until the end of 1872, when it was purchased under powers of an Act of Parliament for £57,300, and formally opened free of toll February 8th, 1873. The original claim for compensation in respect of tolls was set down at £73,832.

Kew is famous for its gardens, for its Physical Observatory, and as the residence of George III. at Kew House. Amusing stories are told of the king and his simple life at his rural retreat. Improvements in the grounds were made by "Capability" Brown, but the decided measures and impatience of interference shown by the famous landscape gardener rather tried the king's temper, and Mason, the poet, tells us that when his Majesty heard of Brown's death, he went to the under gardener, and in a tone of great satisfaction, said "Mellicant, Brown is dead; now you and I can do here as we please."[1]

STRAND-ON-THE-GREEN stretches from Kew Bridge towards Chiswick, to which parish it belongs. It consisted of little more than a collection of fishermen's cottages until the beginning of the eighteenth century, but it then came into favour, and several good residences were built. Among the inhabitants of note may be mentioned Joe Miller, David Mallet, and Zoffany, the Royal Academician. Zoffany used the fishermen of Strand-on-the-Green or Brentford as models for his pictures. When he painted a "Last Supper" as the altar-piece for old Brentford Church, he introduced the features of several of the fishermen with so much success that these men came to be called by the names of the disciples they represented, much to the disgust of the wife of that one who figured as Judas Iscariot.

[1] Walpole's Letters, ed. Cunningham, viii. 367.

Plate 13

PLATE XIII

WIMBLEDON, EAGLE HOUSE

THERE have been many fine old houses in Wimbledon, but few are now left, and Eagle House, the subject of Mr. Way's drawing, is one of these. This Jacobean house remained in private occupation until the end of the eighteenth century, when it was occupied as a school, and so it continued for nearly a century. The present occupier is the well-known architect, Mr. T. G. Jackson, R.A., who pulled down such modern additions as had been built to meet the requirements of a boys' school, and thus allowed the old house to reappear as it was when it was a private residence.

Mr. Jackson showed Eagle House to the members of the Surrey Archæological Society on June 14th, 1890, when he read an interesting paper[1] on its history, from which the following particulars are taken. Mr. Jackson refers to it as one of the few well-preserved examples of the private residence of a London merchant in the reign of James I.

The house does not appear to have had any special name when it was built, before 1613, by Robert Bell, citizen and merchant of London, member of the Girdlers' Company, and afterwards Deputy of Lime Street Ward. Bell was born at Wimbledon in 1564. He appears to have had two elder brothers, and to have experienced the advantage of the custom of the manor of Wimbledon, by which, on the death of the copyholder, the youngest son was the customary heir. The first mention of the house is in a survey of 1617, where it is described as a fair new house belonging to Mr. Bell. Manning and Bray, in their "History of Surrey," describe the Survey as dated 1607, but Mr. Jackson gives the real date as 1617.

[1] Surrey Archæological Collections, vol. x., pp. 151-164.

Bell died in 1639-40, at the age of seventy-six. His widow let the house to a Mr. Berington, and went back to her native county, Essex. She died at Colchester in 1647, directing that her property was to be sold, and desiring to be buried at Wimbledon by the side of her husband. The property was bought in 1647 by Sir Richard Betenson, of Layer de la Hay, in Essex. His grandson, Sir Edward Betenson, sold the Wimbledon property in 1700 to Richard Ivatt, Alderman of London, who enfranchised the copyhold in 1705. The property remained in the family for three generations, when the Ivatts let the house in 1765 to George Bond, who bought it in 1766.

In 1758 it was occupied by William, Viscount Duncannon, and after him by Sir William Draper, the General who is now remembered as one of those vilified by Junius. The last private resident was the Right Hon. William Grenville (who was created Baron Grenville in 1790) and during his short residence he was frequently visited by the great minister, the younger William Pitt. There is a tradition that a room on the first floor, looking into the garden and opening into the library, was Pitt's room.

In 1789 the house and seventeen acres were sold for £2,300 to Mr. Thomas Lancaster, who occupied the house as a school. He probably let part of the land for building purposes, as a little street that runs by the east side of the garden is named Lancaster Place. Lancaster was a friend of Lord Nelson, and, in honour of the great admiral, he named his school Nelson House. Nelson and Lady Hamilton, who were then living at Merton, frequently visited Nelson House School.

The school was kept successively by Messrs. Stoughton and Mayer, Mayer and Brackenbury, and, finally, by the Rev. Dr. Huntingford, who gave the house its present name. Dr. Huntingford had previously kept a school at Eagle House, Hammersmith, and when he came to Wimbledon, he brought with him the eagle which now surmounts the middle gable of the front.

Mr. Jackson's paper is illustrated by a view of the garden front of Eagle House. Mr. Way's drawing shows the front to the road.

PLATE XIV

PUTNEY HIGH STREET

NOT many years ago Putney was a "happy hunting-ground" for picturesque old buildings, but unfortunately most of them have now disappeared. The two houses in Mr. Way's drawing are among the few that remain. It would appear from the character of the building with two wings, that these two houses once formed one mansion. The division must, however, have been made at an early period, as the hooded canopies to the doors date the change when the one house was made into two.

One of the most distinguished natives of Putney was Thomas Cromwell, Henry VIII.'s powerful minister, who obtained the name of *malleus monachorum*. Cromwell's father was a blacksmith at Putney, and in the Survey of Wimbledon Manor, taken in 1617, mention is made of "an ancient cottage called the smith's shop lying west of the highway leading from Putney to the upper gate, and on the south side of the highway from Richmond to Wandsworth being the sign of the Anchor." This may have been the elder Cromwell's forge. When Cromwell came into power he obtained the Manor of Wimbledon (which included Putney), but after his execution it went to the Crown and was subsequently given to the Cecil family.

Oliver Cromwell had his headquarters at Putney in 1647, when the generals held their councils in the church, and sat round the communion table.

The ferry at Putney is mentioned in Domesday Book as yielding a toll of 20s. per annum to the lord of the manor, and is also referred to in the household expenses of Edward I. A bridge to supersede the ferry was proposed in 1671, but the City opposed the scheme, and it was negatived in Parliament. An Act of Parliament was procured, 12 Geo. I., for building a bridge of wood across the Thames from Putney to Fulham, which was begun and finished in 1729 by Mr. Philips, carpenter to George II., at the expense of £23,975. The work was undertaken by thirty subscribers, who advanced the sum of £740 each. These proprietors purchased the ferry (which on an average produced £400 a year), for the sum of £8,000. The Duchess of Marlborough received £364 10s. for her interest in the ferry as lady of the manor of Wimbledon. The Bishop of London received £23 for his interest in the Fulham side, besides which he reserved to himself and his household, and to his successors, the right of passing the bridge toll-free.

The old wooden bridge was cleared away, and the building of a new and handsome stone bridge was undertaken by the Metropolitan Board of Works. The memorial stone was laid July 12th, 1884, by the Prince and Princess of Wales, who also opened the bridge to the public on June 4th, 1886. The cost was nearly £250,000, or including the value of the property which it was necessary to acquire in order to make proper approaches, £300,000.

PLATE XV

ALBERT HOUSE, SOUTH STREET, WANDSWORTH

THE rural original of the name of Wandsworth—the village of the river Wandle—does not describe very accurately the present town-like appearance of the place. Wandsworth is too near London to retain much of a country character, and it is now filled with factories, mills and miscellaneous works. The manufacturing element entered early into the economy of the village: thus Aubrey relates that before his time there had been established at Wandsworth a manufacture of "brass plates for kettles, skellets, frying-pans, etc., by Dutchmen who keep it a mystery." · The houses where this was established were long known as the "Frying-pan houses."

Few picturesque old houses are left in Wandsworth, but the curious old building shown in Mr. Way's drawing, is one of these few. One of the special characteristics of this house is to be found in the elaborately carved wood brackets which support the upper part of the building. It appears to have been built early in the seventeenth century, and an inscription on the front gives the exact date as 1620.

What was the original name cannot be affirmed with certainty, but there can be no doubt that "Albert House" is a modern one.

Plate 16

PLATE XVI

CLAPHAM COMMON, NORTH SIDE

CLAPHAM COMMON has ever been one of the most pleasing of the southern suburbs, and its character is well described in the expression—"the villa-cinctured common." Many of the fine old houses, such as that one which was built for Bishop Gauden and lived in by Sir Dennis Gauden, and afterwards by W. Hewer and his friend Samuel Pepys, have been pulled down.

The great philosopher, Henry Cavendish, styled the "Newton of Chemistry," lived in a house which is now re-fronted and altered. The name of Cavendish Road is due to this residence of Henry Cavendish.

There is considerable inequality in the appearance of the houses in this drawing, but they harmonize with the trees and the shrubs, and go to form an effective picture of an important portion of the surroundings of this famous common. This row, numbering 12 to 23, North Side, was formerly known as Church Buildings.

Plate 17

PLATE XVII

FAIRFIELD HOUSE, TOOTING

THIS fine old mansion, which is an ornament to the otherwise commonplace suburb of Tooting, appears to have been built in 1633. We may assume this from that date appearing on an inscribed stone now in the garden, but which once formed a part of the house.

It has not always borne the name of Fairfield House, but was called at one time the " White House." Some fifty years or more ago the house was occupied as a boy's school and was known as Dr. Lord's Academy. Dr. Lord added to the house for the purposes of his school. The freehold of the house, with its large garden behind, was lately bought by the Chelsea Vestry for the purpose of a suburban workhouse to relieve the pressure on their Chelsea workhouse. There is a large panelled entrance hall and a grand staircase. Both the front and the back doors are surmounted by a splendid canopy, the one over the front door being shown in the drawing.

The entrance gate is also worthy of special notice.

Plate 18

PLATE XVIII

THE BROCKLEY JACK, BROCKLEY

NOT many years ago, before railways made them accessible, Brockley and New Cross were very rural places, and fields were common in their neighbourhood. Now the number of houses is daily increasing, and little or nothing of the country remains.

One of the last relics of past times, the wayside inn in the Brockley Road, was cleared away two years ago. Tradition says that an inn has stood on the site of the Brockley Jack for nigh on four centuries, but tradition does not help us to any trustworthy information respecting its history, and the sign could hardly have been given to it before the seventeenth or the eighteenth century.

Anecdotes of highwaymen are more common on the north side of the river than on the south, but there were a considerable number of these gentry in the south. The open country and protecting woods were favourable to their attacks upon property, particularly as coaches and carriages on the great southern road were very numerous.

Brockley Jack is said to have been the name of one of these highwaymen, but whether this be so or not, there is little doubt that the old inn was frequented by gentlemen of the road. There was a particular staircase so constructed that it could be removed at night, and thus cut off access to the upper storey, in the case of criminals being secreted there.

The inn was a long low house with a bay window looking on to the front garden, built and added to at different times. In the garden were rows of seats and tables beneath old trees, and a large but almost branchless stump carried the signboard.

A penthouse on one side sheltered some of the seats, and on the other was an outside staircase leading to the upper floor of an annexe built at right angles to the main building. The history of the Brockley Jack is very vague, and little can be recorded of it with any certainty. Now that it has been cleared away, the memory of the associations which clung around its old buildings to the last, will probably soon be forgotten.

Plate 19

PLATE XIX

COLFE'S ALMSHOUSES, LEWISHAM

THE Rev. Abraham Colfe, Vicar of Lewisham, was a considerable benefactor to this place. In his lifetime he founded a grammar school for thirty-one boys on Blackheath (within the parish of Lewisham) which was opened in the month of June, 1652, and also an English school at Lewisham. He bequeathed a certain sum of money to be laid out in building five almshouses (to be begun in the month of April, 1662) for poor godly householders of Lewisham parish of sixty years of age or upwards, and able to say the Creed, the Lord's Prayer, and the Ten Commandments. The Leathersellers' Company added a sixth almshouse.

The Trustees of the Lewisham Charities have the right to nominate five persons to the almshouses, the inmate of the remaining almshouse being appointed from poor freemen of the Leatherseller's Company, or their widows or daughters. Candidates must be single persons of either sex, poor and impotent, of good character, who are not and have not at any time within two years next preceding been in receipt of parochial relief. Inmates receive five shillings a week and medical attendance.

These picturesque buildings on the west side of the village, and to the south of the old church, are of great interest, and show how much more capable the old builders were of giving distinction and architectural effect to commonplace buildings than their successors in the present day.

Over the door are the arms of the founder and of the Leathersellers' Company, and the following inscription :

"Año decimo sexto Caroli 2. Año Dni. 1664. The gift of Mr. Abraham Colfe, late Vicar of this parish, whereof the Company of Leathersellers in London are according to the desire of his will by Act of Parliament appointed governors, and by the said Company the gift is enlarged."

The Rev. A. Colfe went first to reside at Lewisham as curate to Dr. Hadrianus Sadriana in 1604, and in 1610 he was presented to the vicarage.

Plate 20

PLATE XX

CHARLTON HOUSE

CHARLTON HOUSE, Kent, is a most interesting old palatial residence, and, like Holland House, Kensington, is a grand relic of the fine domestic architecture of the early part of the seventeenth century. Considering its near neighbourhood to London, it is astonishing that it should have remained in so fine condition to our own time.

This, the manor-house, was commenced in 1607 by Sir Adam Newton, tutor to Henry, Prince of Wales, and completed in 1612. It is said to be the work of Inigo Jones, and there is considerable reason to believe that the tradition is true. Mr. Thorne ("Environs of London") says that Jones lived at Charlton in a house built by himself, and afterwards known as Cherry Garden Farm, and also that Charlton House is strikingly like Charlton in Wilts (Earl of Suffolk's), which was built by Inigo Jones about the same time.

John Evelyn was a great friend of Sir Henry Newton, and mentions in his Diary his several visits to Charlton and he tells us that the house was originally built for Prince Henry, and this is an additional reason for attributing the design to Inigo Jones, for he was architect to Prince Henry. On May 30th, 1652, Evelyn wrote, "In the afternoone to Charlton Church, where I heard a Rabinical sermon. Here is a faire monument in black marble of Sir Adam Newton, who built that faire house neere it, for Prince Henry, and where my noble friend, Sir Henry Newton, succeeded him."

He again wrote, on June 9th, 1653, "I went to visit my worthy neighbour, Sir Hen. Newton, and consider the prospect which is doubtless for city, river, ships, meadows, hill, woods, and all other amenities, one of the most noble in the world; so as had ye house running water, it were a princely seate."

Charlton House is built of red brick and stone, the plan that of a capital E, with projecting wings and porch. There is a turret at each end, and a balustrade along the whole front, hiding the roof. The interior has a large central hall, panelled with oak, and a chapel adjoining the principal dining-room. This was consecrated in the year 1616.

Sir William Ducie (afterwards Viscount Downe) bought the house from Sir Henry Newton, and made considerable alterations in 1659. Evelyn visited him on August 16th, 1664, and notes the occurrence in his Diary: "I went to Sir Wm. Ducie's house at Charlton, which he purchased of my excellent friend, Sir Henry Newton, now nobly furnished."

In the year 1742 Charlton House was in the occupation of John, second Earl of Egmont, who formed here a valuable library. His celebrated son, Spencer Perceval, afterwards Prime Minister, spent some of his earlier years at Charlton House, and subsequently married Jane, the daughter of the owner of the house, Sir Thomas Spencer Wilson, son-in-law of Margaretta Maria Maryon, the rich heiress, who married John Badger Weller. The two names of Maryon and Wilson are now borne by the present owner.

In Charlton Church there is a tablet by Chantrey to the memory of Spencer Perceval, Prime Minister, who was shot in the lobby of the House of Commons, May 11th, 1812. The church and churchyard are rich in other memorials to celebrated men. The early fellows of the Royal Society, Henry Oldenburg, and Robert Hooke, who did so much for the promotion of science, both died at Charlton, and the former was buried in the churchyard, but without a monument.

Plate 21

PLATE XXI

MORDEN COLLEGE, BLACKHEATH

MORDEN COLLEGE, in Charlton parish, is one of the most charming old red-brick buildings in the neighbourhood of London. It is a square building, with lofty entrance gateway inclosing a quadrangle, and having lodgings, dining-hall and chapel. It is the work of Strong, the master-mason of St. Paul's, who erected it in 1694, and it does great credit to his artistic ability. The red brick is treated with stone quoins and dressings. There was originally a canal in front of the building, which is shown in some of the old prints of the place, but this was drained when the North Kent Railway was carried under the grounds by a tunnel, and the excavated sand was used to form the undulating lawn. There is also a pretty garden behind.

This college was founded by Sir John Morden, Bart., a wealthy Turkey merchant, who built the house in 1694, as already stated, near his own mansion. Sir John kept twelve decayed merchants here, and by his will, dated October 15th, 1702, bequeathed to the College, upon the decease of his wife, all his real and copyhold estates for the maintenance of poor and aged merchants of England, whose fortunes had been ruined by perils of the sea or other unavoidable accidents, preference being given to those who had traded with the Levant. Sir John died in 1708, and Lady Morden was unable to continue her husband's bounty to the twelve merchants. She was therefore obliged during her lifetime to reduce the number to four. She died in 1721, when the whole estate fell to the College. The property has greatly increased in value, and the original scheme has been extended. There are now a chaplain and about forty pensioners, who, besides lodging, maintenance and attendance, have each an annual stipend of £72. The pensioners must be upwards of fifty years of age, bachelors or widowers, and members of the Church of England.

Over the entrance are statues of the founder and his wife. Their portraits are also in the hall and their arms in the chapel, where they were buried.

Plate 22

Plate 23

Plate 24

PLATES XXIII AND XXIV

GREENWICH

THERE are in all four views of Greenwich, that of Greenwich Hospital commences the present volume, and three—Croom's Hill and Stockwell Street, High Bridge, and the Ranger's Lodge —end it.

The town of Greenwich, with its hospital, park and observatory is one of the most interesting suburbs of London, from its wealth of historical associations.

The town itself has grown up to its present size from a small fishing village. The supply of whitebait made it famous centuries ago, and its fish dinners have made it a favourite resort up to our own time. The Ministerial fish dinners are supposed to have originated in the banquets given at the Palace to the Council during their sittings. In later times the "Ship" was the resort of the Conservative Ministers and the "Trafalgar" of the Liberals.

The first notice of the "Ship" is in 1634, and there is a token of the house extant with the representation of a ship in full sail, and the legend "Ship Tavern, 1640." There has always been a good supply of hotels and inns in Greenwich. In the middle of the eighteenth century the "Greyhound" was the chief house, and at the beginning of the nineteenth century it was replaced by the "Crown and Sceptre," to be succeeded in this position by the "Ship." The "Trafalgar" is a comparatively modern house.

Croom's Hill has been supposed by some to mean crooked, as these writers derive its name from the Anglo-Saxon word *crumb*. The drawing shows the commencement of the hill, upon which were built several houses of some importance. The house of the Mason family was at the top of Croom's Hill, on the west side. It was built by William Smith, whose widow, Alice (*née* Duppa), sold the property to Robert Mason, D.C.L., in 1634. Dr. Mason writing on March 17th, 1636-7, to Sir Edward Nicholas, invited the Secretary of State to his "Hermitage at Greenwich," if he should accompany the Court to the Palace there. Evelyn went to see the house on September 25th, 1652, on account of the prospect for which it was famous, but he describes the house itself as a wretched one.

Sir William Hooker, Lord Mayor, 1673, purchased property on Croom's Hill and lived there.

When the Dowager Duchess of Brunswick became a resident of Brunswick House (afterwards the Ranger's Lodge), her medical attendant, Daniel Peter Layard, M.D., purchased a house on Croom's Hill.

STOCKWELL STREET, seen in the middle distance of the drawing, has a number of very quaint old houses of small size, several being "weather tiled" with wood.

HIGH BRIDGE is the name of part of a narrow alley running at the back of the "Trafalgar," and ending at the old Trinity Hospital for Mercantile Seamen. The buildings are mostly wooden, and those on the riverside, chiefly occupied by small builders and letters of pleasure boats.

www.ingramcontent.com/pod-product-compliance
Lightning Source LLC
Chambersburg PA
CBHW030403170426
43202CB00010B/1474